GOLDEN CHILD

by Mark Ravenhill

samuelfrench.co.uk

FOR AMATEUR PRODUCTION ENQUIRIES

UNITED KINGDOM AND WORLD
EXCLUDING NORTH AMERICA
plays@samuelfrench.co.uk
020 7255 4302/01

Each title is subject to availability from Samuel French,
depending upon country of performance.

THINKING ABOUT PERFORMING A SHOW?

There are thousands of plays and musicals available to perform from Samuel French right now, and applying for a licence is easier and more affordable than you might think

From classic plays to brand new musicals, from monologues to epic dramas, there are shows for everyone.

Plays and musicals are protected by copyright law, so if you want to perform them, the first thing you'll need is a licence. This simple process helps support the playwright by ensuring they get paid for their work and means that you'll have the documents you need to stage the show in public.

Not all our shows are available to perform all the time, so it's important to check and apply for a licence before you start rehearsals or commit to doing the show.

LEARN MORE & FIND THOUSANDS OF SHOWS

Browse our full range of plays and musicals, and find out more about how to license a show
www.samuelfrench.co.uk/perform

Talk to the friendly experts in our Licensing team for advice on choosing a show and help with licensing
plays@samuelfrench.co.uk   020 7387 9373

Acting Editions

BORN TO PERFORM

Playscripts designed from the ground up to work the way you do in rehearsal, performance and study

---

Larger, clearer text for easier reading

Wider margins for notes

Performance features such as character and props lists, sound and lighting cues, and more

---

+ CHOOSE A SIZE AND STYLE TO SUIT YOU

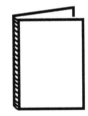

STANDARD EDITION

Our regular paperback book at our regular size

SPIRAL-BOUND EDITION

The same size as the Standard Edition, but with a sturdy, easy-to-fold, easy-to-hold spiral-bound spine

LARGE EDITION

A4 size and spiral bound, with larger text and a blank page for notes opposite every page of text – perfect for technical and directing use

---

LEARN MORE | **samuelfrench.co.uk/actingeditions**

Other plays by MARK RAVENHILL
published and licensed by Samuel French

Candide

Citizenship

Ghost Story

Handbag

Mother Clap's Molly House

Over There

Pool (No Water)

Product

Scenes from Family Life

Shoot/Get Treasure/Repeat

Shopping and Fucking

Some Explicit Polaroids

The Cut

The Experiment

FIND PERFECT PLAYS TO PERFORM AT
www.samuelfrench.co.uk/perform

ABOUT THE AUTHOR

Mark Ravenhill was born in Haywards Heath, West Sussex in 1966. He studied Drama and English at Bristol University. His first play *Shopping and Fucking* was produced by Out of Joint and the Royal Court Theatre in 1996. Subsequent plays include *Faust Is Dead* and *Handbag* (both Actors Touring Company), *Some Explicit Polaroids* (Out of Joint at the Ambassadors Theatre), *Mother Clap's Molly House* and *Citizenship* (both National Theatre), *Pool (No Water)* (Frantic Assembly at the Lyric Theatre), *The Cut* (Donmar Theatre), *Shoot/Get Treasure/ Repeat* (Paines Plough) and *Over There* (Royal Court). From 2012 to 2014, Mark was playwright in residence for the Royal Shakespeare Company, producing a new version of Brecht's *Galileo* and *Candide* inspired by Voltaire (both Swan Theatre, Stratford-Upon-Avon). Mark's work in music theatre includes a new English version of Monteverdi's *The Coronation of Poppea* with additional material by Michael Nyman (King's Head); *Ten Plagues*, a song cycle for Marc Almond with composer Connor Mitchell (Traverse Theatre) and *Elysium* with composer Rolf Wallin for the Norwegian Opera. Mark is the co-creator of the ITV sitcom *Vicious*.

MUSIC USE NOTE

Licensees are solely responsible for obtaining formal written permission from copyright owners to use copyrighted music in the performance of this play and are strongly cautioned to do so. If no such permission is obtained by the licensee, then the licensee must use only original music that the licensee owns and controls. Licensees are solely responsible and liable for all music clearances and shall indemnify the copyright owners of the play(s) and their licensing agent, Samuel French, against any costs, expenses, losses and liabilities arising from the use of music by licensees. Please contact the appropriate music licensing authority in your territory for the rights to any incidental music.

IMPORTANT BILLING AND CREDIT REQUIREMENTS

If you have obtained performance rights to this title, please refer to your licensing agreement for important billing and credit requirements.

FIRST PERFORMANCE INFO

GOLDEN CHILD was commissioned by the Lyric Theatre, Hammersmith and first presented at the Roundabout Theatre, Summerhall, as part of the Edinburgh Festival, August 2014.

CHARACTERS

A
B
C
D
E
F

The first production used three actors

1.

B Last night

A Don't remember

B you

A I was monged

B last night yes you were monged so

A Want to be call my dealer

B no last we you listen Last night you we drove in to the favela

A My

B new your birthday car and

A played?

B Yes we did yes we delete the chav

A My dealer's not

B You you hit a chav

A I

B in the favela last night in the

A Yes?

B Yes

A An adult?

B Forty fifty

A An adult a fucking Yes! Did you record?

B Then you

A Fuck why didn't? Doesn't count it's not

B but

A Fucking 'nother what fucking holiday

B You got out the car

A In the favela?

B You got out the car in the

A Fuck must have been

B the chav you said still

A Wouldn't

B exactly count. going to like a kindness wring the neck. get down in the like there's mud and like over your

A call your dealer

B jeans. reached out to the chav

A you call your dealer

B so there's chav blood all over *(later)* mud and blood

A if I'm not monged there's gonna be

B the chav was I was rear view-mirror chav's mouth's moving you listen held cradled

A cradled?

B cradled

A just grubby

B no

A the chav's? fuck never do anything hate myself my life's a chav alive

B Listen want to: you're cradling the chav, the mouth's moving you

A swim in the pool

B pulled the chav's head up your ear

A don't want to swim in the

B and that's when this is the important chav whispers something in your ear can you remember?

A yes

B you can remember?

A yes

B what did the

A Chav whispered in my ear: "don't want to die never know what it felt like. please—"

B yes?

A "up the arse and cum in my"

B O you why do I even retard

A call your dealer

B fallen out with my

A fuck

B going to tell because I know you're my best I really

A okay

B you come back to the car drive nobody's going to let us in to you're covered in the mud blood so you pull a parking lot and you weep

A I never

B I know

A Not an emotional how can I? This is no a story you're

B That's when I see recorded so

A I'm not want to

B Listen you have to listen

A *(recorded sobbing)* Who am I?

   Why am I so?

B There's what twenty minutes over over over the chav whispered put this sadness inside and you Remember any?

A No

B Don't believe you

A Why would I?

B I know you when you and you're you're You know what the chav whispered Listen it's We're all inside all of us there's this big sadness if we don't we have to let it yes? I need you to remember

2.

A Last night

C Don't need to know about

A This is

C Your time When we have our time then we

A I hit a chav

C I love you I forgive you
    It doesn't What's the average fourteen fifteen?

A Don't want to

C Someone's been putting these in your Some friend told you
    a story and you

A Chav in the mud jeans covered in

C Your jeans are clean

A Holding the chav as

C I saw the maid take your jeans to the and

A maybe she washed away the

C your jeans were clean and that was a story and you are silly
    silly silly Listen: our life up here perfection

A Yes

C Everything we make up stories Something beast in doesn't
    want the the

A Maybe that's

C Like : your father walks back through the door after all these
    he's still the same and he unwraps the bundle and there's
    the heart he's cut out the heart of that and he says: I never
    loved that whore thought but I never and now I've cut her
    and I've come back to be with you and my

A You actually

C play that in Yes So if you need to make up some then I
understand Skinny dipping? Feeling all the water on you
in you that's

A I

C All happiness

A I want you to listen to : WHO AM I? See chav whispered I
drove but sobbing

C Darling are you unhappy?

A I don't I

C I don't want you to be unhappy

A I am yes I am yes unhappy

C Oh darling

A there's like a sadness inside great big which I

C If you want to talk to

A I want to talk to

C I can pay for

A If I can talk to the chav Just find the chav and ask the chav
what they whispered and

C A person in a no blood on the jeans a story

A 'til Tell me about the day I was born

C The pool looks lonely

A never talk about the Tell me about the day I was

C painful for me

A Surely you can remember

C All you need to know: the past was horrible present is happy.
Look about maid pool car camera all you where are you?

A call the hospitals

C silly

A call around the have to know if

C They don't even have hospitals for Why are you? Do you want
to be unhappy? Want me to? I'm old stupid I know and you
don't and I you leave the past or you will be unhappy and
that's why come on the pool or mong or

A Phoning every hospital 'til

3.

A Last night you were hit in the favela

D Don't remember

A Last night kid drove in to the favela hit you

D Doctor says I'll never

A lying in the mud your lung was your leg

D got a nice place up there?

A You were the only one brought in last night from the only one hit by the

D you want me to forgive? Why should I? You're

A This hospital how much are you? Because I can pay for this is shit they'll kill you in this

D Good people

A good people good won't Do you want to live? You've got a child grandchild? See this? See how much money ? With this you can live. Last night in the favela

D Visiting my child grandchild

A Which?

D Both I

A You have to be

D I'll

A accurate if you want the you've got to be

D one minute walking suddenly in the but knew quickly the game I've been before by a kid in the

A I'm sorry

D If you want me to forgive I'll

A No no. Tell me what—

D You came to me kneeled in the you I remember held

A You do you

D Of course I

A remember

D Saw blood on your jeans thinking: So much. Where does the? my blood

A Your blood on my?

D All over

A So why did the mai—? Bitch

D You want me to?

A Carry on

D You reminded me of...no

A Carry on

D I can't there's no more I can't when there's no

A Listen This isn't a hospital This is a hut with a few charity Have you seen? Blood shit on the. Here you're going to

D My memory is You drove in to my Broke my and you want

A die you sad cunt goodbye to granny Twenty dollars for a hole in the ground Okay I recorded got back drove then recorded WHO AM I? Something Here I'll I hold you it's a trigger hold you You reach out to me Whisper You were seen the rear-view mirror you whispered and

D No

A Don't. You put this infected sadness it won't until you

D It's not

A I'll pay for the hospital your daughter to move to an apartment your grandchild the university.

D You are not who you think you are. Your parents are not your parents

A That's what you?

D Your parents are not your parents. Yes. Shall I tell you the whole?

A Yes

D It's expensive

A Money is no object

D I was a maid. Your parents

A My real

D parents yes were Your mother a mayor. Your father a professor politics. When the coup You know there was a

A No one ever

D No one talks about the coup anymore

A When was?

D Your mother father opposed so they took you away from your parents. Taken away forever and they

A ...

D Shall

A Making me like something sad

D Just beginning Where are you?

A For a drive

D Coming back?

A No

D Inside you now. Only I can You'll come back

A I don't need CHAV SCUM

D Give me the money

A I'm not

D I need the money

A I corrupted Sorry Offered money and you course offered lies

D Every word I speak is

A I pay you nothing what will you tell me?

D truth costs just as much as

A No money

D You'll never

A I'll If they're true remember for myself

4.

B What did the chav

A My

B say?

A Listen I

B Yes?

A need to leave this is my

B not

A Can't your voice in my

B you

A Just Get monged go to some

B this unhappiness I'm not WHO AM I?

A I'll sit Remember When it's all then I just

B all the time in the

A ...

B ...

A there's no I'm a blank blank Go back told the chav I

B Don't need the chav

A Offer enough money

B What did the?

A It's not

B Tell me

A You are not who you think you are. Your parents are not your real parents.

B Who were your real did the chav?

A can't so just

B Sometimes my parents checking NASDAQ or or or watching the I: don't belong didn't like some memory deep in My parents are not my parents Same for You're not alone I'm here the same

A ...

B Who were the real? What did the?

A One day the a coup

B No one's ever

A Don't talk anymore about the But there

B yes the now I distant but yes the coup

A You remember?

B remember the living happy. One day the coup regime came to Mummy and Daddy

A My mummy was a mayor. Daddy professor politics it was

B What was my mummy? Can't

A "nascent proletarian power"

B What does that some?

A "nascent proletarian power"

B What language?

A Daddy's I'm like so supper Adults eight ten Smoke cigars and Daddy's holding Authority in Everyone argue debate laughing Daddy's in and that's what he nascent proletarian

B doesn't

A But

B exist. It's not

A It's a I've fantasised the whole

B no

A because doesn't everyone fantasise some Hate myself

B   it's a real We feel a real just because that

A   why are there no?

B   must have Words don't want us If they want us to forget
They've

A   Yes Deleted everything that doesn't Past wiped and they've Lies

B   Never trust ever

A   All we have's Got to remember The coup and

B   What did they?

A   Remember remember

B   It's like It's there Almost on my but still can't

A   There's others

B   The chav said

A   Taken away from Can't be just you me

B   Might be

A   There'll be

B   only us

A   Thousands tens of got to be

B   My feeling's you and me

A   Together if we come togeth and we together you see remember

B   Who you going to?

A   Shout out 'til

B   If nobody comes you'll be

A   There'll be others. They'll come.

5.

B I remember yes it was a carpet place where they

E Carpet factory?

B It was a carpet factory there's a smell which was dye they used to the yes and Mummy was a I was taken so little I was taken to the place where they made the and Mummy was

E Worker?

B Mummy was she organised spoke on behalf of There was a meeting and Mummy she was speaking on behalf of the and she

E My daddy was a Drove a bus. In the evening there'd be meetings The House Everyone bring food

A Smoking

E Maybe

A You remember the smoking of cigars?

E I

A Everyone back then

B Yes I remember now they yes smoked cigars

A And you do you?

E I don't know if Daddy

A Everyone smoked cigars

E Then yes I suppose yes Daddy must have yes smoked cigars And Daddy said: We're strong now but they won't stand for they won't let this

A Nascent proletarian power

E I don't

A Did Daddy use the words?

E I don't remember the no he

A Those were important in those nascent proletarian. That's what my dad

E My daddy never to my

A You have to remember accurately If you can't You should stay silent

B ...

A My daddy had

B Yes

A They our daddies had authority

B And my mummy too she had Coup

E Yes everyone that's what they Everyone smoking debating There'll be a coup important when the time came to build a – they had a word—

B Guns

E That's not the

B Mummy told the carpet factory: We are not violent in our natures but when the time comes we have to be prepared to

E Barricades

B We have to shoot

A What's a barri—?

B Everyone argued but Mummy she: that's the reality

A I remember now one day waking up opening the there were tanks. Does everyone remember the?

B Yes

A coming down the streets. Over the square crushing the flowers in the

E Yes There were tanks because the coup had

B Mummy said they have a list

A They were all on the Our mummies and daddies were all on the list because they were going to be what? What?

E Don't know can't

A There must have been a

E Questioned

B Exterminated

E Taken to a place where they were going to be

B Blindfolded shot

E Interrogated

B no they didn't this was a coup they didn't

E remember definitely interro

B Shot Don't tell me my

A Hey some were interrogated some shot some interrogated then shot different they can't okay

B What's your memory?

A Mummy was a mayor Daddy was a professor politics. Took them away and they were. Not shot not interrogated. I was told they were there's a word word they used what's the word got to remember the anyone remember the?

B Take your

A Can't

B slowly

A Sorry I'm a user actually need thought I'd I called this meeting and now all I just want to be

E We all use that's

A You're a user?

B That's what they've done to us

A Deranged that's the word deranged They weren't shot interrogate they were deranged Remember

E I was wrong you're right deranged

A Do you?

B heard a gun firing Mummy's screams

A No they came to us told us: We are taking your mummy and daddy away their mental instability is a threat to the new social order which is necessary for the prosperity of our remember that?

E I remember that very clearly now

B sure I heard the gun

A They were classified deranged taken away to a

E An asylum

A I suppose if they were then yes a

B Former university now classified as an asylum

A Taken to

E Yes taken in to the university asylum to the ward cell classroom where Mummy Daddy

A Held me held really so tight actually thought killing squeezing the life out of

B Goodbye my darling

A Then through the other door the new

E The new mummy daddy parent of the new regime came take us away up to the big house new life begin

B why did they do/

A I suppose

B Why would they want?

E It was must policy the new regime

A Like a yes charitable act of the

E Wives of the new regime come

B Adopt a child of the deranged

A Take away our past memories of the

E Tearing down the banners in the brain that's what they

A Yes

E Tearing down the banners in the

A And so the children were taken away by their new
mummies and daddies who owned the gas TV the docks
telecommunications all the children forgot

B made to forget

A the old parents living out their lives wealth happiness

B supposed happiness

E false

B lies

A I'm angry at the There is this big anger inside at all the
wrong that has been

E There must be truth

B Justice

E One thing at a

B We'll demand

E Truth

A What we must Each of us We must accuse Return accuse the
false parents All the lies All these years now you must tell
me the truth That's what each of us must do.

6.

A You are not my mother You are a false

C Why must you

A mother. You took me away there was a coup you

C If you want to if that's the

A took me up here

C game we're playing

A you have filled me with your

C not a very good but if the story we

A Story I'm not talking about the you cunt

C talk like a chav

A you are a cunt tells everything all this is lies stolen from the you took all this from the people you tanks

C when I've swum we'll

A you will why can't you can't tell me the truth

C did you fall out with your?

A until you

C dealer? Is that why?

A use for once that cunt mouth to speak the truth

C I know a friend with a dealer I if that's what I'll

A The day I was born

C prepared to step beyond the law if that

A You can't even tell me about

C Difficult for me

A Of course yes because you weren't even Your womb's you can't even nothing ever from your barren

C   I'll call the

A   I don't belong This isn't my

C   Go fine

A   important not for me the group

C   Ah

A   need to the true stories have to be told or never

C   Knew there must be this group Putting lies in your

A   Unless the It's necessary for me the yes group but also you
    Can't you see? You can't be happy unless you Have to tell
    the truth The coup

C   All

A   You'll tell the truth?

C   I'll tell the truth

A   The day I was born

C   The day you were born was the time was broken whole country
    was They'd eating propaganda The people are good But all
    this Politics They were children didn't under We'll take over
    the factory Everything free give all the wealth Everyone
    taking nobody making money We had to You're right The
    coup a necessary

A   You were the enemy

C   sanity

A   that's why you took

C   didn't take any

A   ripped me from the hand in the asylum you

C   you are mine came from this from inside me

A   don't

C   you were inside me my waters breaking we had to get in to
    the hospital but they'd barricaded that's what they said it

was justice equality but they barricaded the Where's the humanity in that? Your father: Let this woman her baby – you – is coming but they wouldn't The communists wouldn't So that's when Daddy shot Daddy shot in to the Bodies falling It was

A How can

C Why I never you were born in The past was

A CAPITALIST! BEOURGOIS! VAMPIRE! SCUM! Won't believe the lies fed by the bullies who took our! We will rip up the yes paving stones we will knock you you will lie before us but we will not deviate bring the stone down your skull again again again you are wiped until our country is free from the class!

C The group's put

A You will speak only when permission is given.

C These words

A What do you want? Death sentence?

C You're talk and you're not even Do something The paving stone on the skull yes? Hit me. Come on. Hit.

A ...

C It's darling I understand I'm your natural Where?

A The group

C Talking? We did The coup We acted You can't even hit No child of mine

7.

B We each

A difficult

B Report to the group if we

A Listen I don't belong in the

B If you don't

A This is not the place for

B Hey

A Worthless

E It's not Nothing's My so-called-father laughed I'm accusing him of and he

B Did your mother she laughed?

A I

E you're infantile I said rather infantile than

A Yes

E sprayed over the walls the OUR WORLD AND WE WILL OWN IT

B it's everyone was laughed

E Won't be able wash

B I shouted Did you?

A I

B let out the?

A educate her

B yes?

A softly Nascent proletarian power

E not going back Can't live

A Thought she but

E form a camp tents

A She didn't listen

E Start another in our

B yes

E community new values

B to the square then we can Because still so many others

E stolen children

B Call upon all the thousands tens thousands who were

A Listen

E The lies will fall Truth told

B New world made in the

A Listen

E True values true parents Make it

A Listen

B a better

A I shot my mother

   Pause.

   She was given drew up the charges I read out the The people
   find that you She stood before me mouth Lies lies lies spoke
   softly: nothing will move forward long as you But still she
   verdict had to be She was

E Did you

A On behalf of you us I found her

E kill your?

A Held the gun "There's still If you'll just confess"

E *(laughs)*

A Don't you

E *(laughs)*

A No laughter fucking Three bullets straight in Blood over my Had to the pool Clean myself of her

E don't believe you

A Tent that's you think that's That's fucking That'll be two days three think they'll water cannon and you will yes washed away

E It's a real thing

A Real is I've done After what they We all You Kill your false mother Kill your false father

E Deranged Kill

A you're just They're inside your

E This was a place where each of us freely

A You're not with against us

E This is Not part of your

    E *leaves.*

A It's there you see if you look under the see?

B I

A My mother's Washed for hours still under my Can you see?

B What did it like feel?

A not an emotional

B finally the false parent is

A Happy I'm now hap yes

B heroic

A Yes

B I've Only I couldn't All talk but you

A Well

   Kiss.

B One day I'll kill

A Listen that was As long as the lies stop don't all

B Want to

A Killing's not the important

B Real mother had a gun in my blood

A important thing: liberate the deranged Doors of the asylum
   open They'll be free Great crowd of the stolen Calling: Here!
   Real mother united with real child, the true father touching
   again his Learn from each other The old ways become the
   new ways We'll topple this and we will build

B want to sleep with you

A Tonight?

8.

B Owe so much my dealer won't

A Fuck the We don't need

B You're not using?

A I'm not using

B But we're both

A well

B Supposed to be us and you

A Better

B on your own

A For us. Better is: liberate the deranged Doors of the asylum open They'll be free Great crowd of the stolen Calling: Here! Real /mother united with real child, the true father touching again his

B Always the yeah blah words blah That doesn't always the same None of it means

A That's what we

B I'm going to steal

A No

B Some little kid's got to

A Don't need

B Telling me? I am my own person You don't If I choose to

A Important we

B it was important we But it's talk Haven't done Not real What's real is I need

A You love me

B Thought but I You're a talker I'm a user Bad combination Find a dealer Move on

A Yesterday I

B Not listening

A Went to the asylum You're right Too many words So I did I went to the asylum Where the real parents

B Were there?

A Army protecting the Men with guns

B You

A watched Just about When Face at the Deranged face pressing against

B Yes

A my father

B How can

A When it's

B Just a

A Mouth was moving I

B could be anyone

A Daddy my professor of politics calling to

B You musn't

A Liberate me

B all hope but you musn't a blur and you're

A To you yes you you don't If it happened Listen your mother okay? Imagine your mother real if she was Don't you somehow you'd

B yes

A know?

B I would

A   Now got can't just want to get in the liberate him can't wait for so

B   My mother is If your dad then my mother could

A   had my gun I could take them fight my shoot the army away until

B   Want to

A   What's?

B   Mummy told them in the carpet factory years ago: The reality is violence so that's why we need

A   Oh

B   My real mother's gun I don't know much about Is it a good?

A   Very

B   now we can shoot our way in When Mummy sees the way I've

A   I need to be monged If I'm gonna

B   No

A   charge through the Want to be

B   Meet your real father and you're No! Want to be clean when I meet my

A   won't even get that they'll shoot us down

B   Better to have tried and Your father pressing his face day after You're not going to Are you going to?

A   I'm still using

B   I know

A   I've lied about I'm a user

B   Don't need We have to liberate Here Take the Hold it What it's like to How does it?

A   Good

B   You can fire the first shot

A Want you to

B Together It'll be so When they hear the story Way we fought Freed the real parents Whole country will rise up in

A Shoot our way through finally we

9.

A We had to shoot We've killed First one I pulled the trigger Looked so surprised as he fell Thought I'd shit myself

B Blood's hot when it hits Cold now Once you've done it once gets Topple like

A Dominoes

B Skittles We did that for

A You, Daddy

B And for Have you seen my?

F Who

A Want to hold Covered in

F are you?

A Daddy me beneath the

F I don't

A blood there's

F Out of here

A your child.

F I'll call the guards

A Little when they took

F The guards will

A away from you

F Guards!

B Stop him they'll

F GUARDS!

B Shut up old man shut your fucking If I have to shoot again I'll Where's my mother? Tell me where

A Hey Give me the

B My gun

F My son was If I hold you then I'll

A You'll get covered

F Touch smell I'll know if you're

A If I could clean away this

B Hold him

A Don't want Daddy to get

B Doesn't matter Just

F No one's ever

B Let him

  A *and* **F** *embrace.*

F Oh my

A Blood's over you too

F Knew if I A child has a smell And you are

A Daddy

F Son

A You smell of I knew cigars

F Did I smoke?

A the table all the people debating you remember the future of our

B My mother in the factory Do you?

F I remember so

B Her gun a trigger

F little.

A Nascent proletarian power.

F They cut open my head see the?

A Yes

F you see the cut where?

B I can't

F What's wrong with the FUCKING STUPID CHILD great
   knife dig in to my

A Course you see it course

F I'm mad leave me I'm a mad person

B Leave him Look for my

A No not

F Open this mouth: Sewer pours out

A They've made you

F I piss blood shit poison

A You're sane sane sane

F I'm the patient They're the

A world is mad. Made you but you're

F Oh son

A We're here to liberate

F Why isn't the other one holding me? Put down the Come over
   here and hold me now I am authority you will

B Don't want you old man. Want my mother.

F Your mother? Ha! Your mother? Know what they did to
   your mother?

B She's here?

F Your mother was a talker sewed up her mouth Then they
   sewed up her eyes Sewed up her

B You saw them?

F Everyone saw it The news Whole country watched her death.

B Oh. Mother's

F family together. Daddy children. Oh my darlings can you
ever forgive what I—?

B Listen I'm not—

F Such a terrible necessary thing I—

B Your child

F Still the same

A Dad you're confused. I'm

F Always the "You're not my father"

A I'm your child Just me

F You are both

B I'm going I

F One step I'll beat you now as I beat you then. YOU ARE MY
CHILD I AM YOUR FATHER YOU WILL RESPECT ME
YOU WILL OBEY THERE MUST BE ORDER IN THE
WORLD

B I won't be

F My fist is still bigger than yours OBEY!

A Daddy you musn't

F Your mother has no eyes mouth cunt I'm all you Come

A She doesn't

F No fighting

A belong

F Let's just for a moment Peace

...

A Are you crying, Daddy?

F No

A Yes

F Old men sometimes

A Why are you crying?

F you're phantoms in the Mad old man

A Phantoms don't We're real Aren't we we're?

B Real

F But how could you survive the?

A We all survived

F Miracle on God's earth

A They took us away Called you

F Speak when you're spoken too. Want you to: I loved you both. That's important. There were no jobs tried everything but

A You were a professor the

F Daddy's speaking When Daddy speaks you Learn the rules Tried to feed you Begged but no one Stripped the paper off the walls Stuffed it your You couldn't keep it down but still I Had to fill your stomachs You would have died painful It was a kindness to You remember I held you said goodbye?

   Pushed you from the bridge saw the current pull you under. Never imagined you'd ever God was watching

A Daddy that's a false

F eh?

A They put that in your None of that

F I see it I still

A Didn't happen

F So you're I'm mad Are you doctor torturer What are you?

A You were a professor but because you opposed the coup they took away your

F The coup?

A The coup when they

F Yes yes the

B You remember?

F course I Thought they'd cut it out of me something like that you

A the tanks?

F Remember women speaking

B My mother

F Your mother

B women in the factory

F All the women all the Something had to be Without silence what's the We sewed up the women's mouths first good for a while

A Daddy you musn't

F stared at us all day long Can you Every woman all day long accusing you with their

A It didn't

F Eyes. We sewed up their eyes. Every woman had to report to the centre where we

B SHUT!

F All the eyes and mouths Think we'd be happy

B Disgusting old Look at him Look Is that your father?

A I

F their cunts wept moaned and stank.

B Would your?

A No

F Can you stink of a million cunts? No one could rest 'til every last cunt was

A Up up shut him

B No more words old man Nothing

A You are not my father. This is an asylum where you belong. One more word and

F exterminate every last

A I will shoot

B I want to Give me My gun

A You don't EVIL EVIL

B I want to kill the old man

A I'll

  Pause.

F You're ghosts

A Nothing's Everything's Everyone telling stories Why can't something one time? He's a story This place

F Angry ghosts chatter chatter

A You're a story

B No

A going back to the pool

B think that's

A A better story than this one

B Give me back my mother's

A The gun's the only real I'm keeping this.

  A *leaves.*

10.

A I want to

C Quietly

A tell you

C speak very

A I've been

C softly Listen can you hear listen

A ...

C snoring Can you hear that?

A I

C listen harder

A Yes snoring

C Daddy argued all night with the whore Not a wink of Turned up hour ago I said: Don't talk now Sleep then we'll

A I made up a story

C We all

A told the group: I executed you Denounced then shot you

C (laughs)

A Yes. (laughs)

C I like that That's how I Mummy's dead inside Long long All feel a bit don't we? Dead. Will you go back to the?

A Group expelled me. The group's finished. There was no. I made up the group.

C There's lots of choices

A I want to be here

C you can choose story that feels the

A I went to an asylum I spoke to a mad man I

C no! That story's a That's a bad Don't tell me any You musn't make me unhappy Look strong but inside I'm You must never tell that ever ever

A Promise

C There are no words to say how much I love you

A ...

C Your dealer called Told him: Call later

A Thank you

C thought you might want to get What can you smell something?

A Yes

C Is it a nice smell?

A What is it?

C Supper. You me Daddy.

A What is it?

C Ah. Secret.

A What is it?

C Alright I'll Here See what Heart of the whore. He did just as I Cut it brought it in a bloody said to the maid: Onions, peppers, brandy splash we'll Just waiting for Daddy to I can hear him Up Showering Soon be in his

A Daddy's going to be there?

C Everything's Don't you want? I'll tell you the secret. This world you say it, makes it so. say:

A I'm happy

C now you're yes

A I'm happy

C you've made it so. And I'm happy.

A Tell me the day I was born

C I'm not going to

A But if I can't

C make up your own one that makes you happy everything will
   be you tell me: Story of the day I was born

A Story of the day I was born: The gods looked upon the child
   they were to send in to the world. saw this child is most
   perfect beautiful child we will ever send and

C that's a lovely

A child is too strong for the favela this child must be sent to
   the most perfect place on the earth the pool is always clean,
   maid obedient, be presented with a new car every

C it's a happy story

A birthday. The angels carried the baby down in to the city
   where Mummy and Daddy sat by the pool praying as they'd
   prayed for years. The bundle was open they wept for...

C Yes?

A ...

C Are you going to finish the?

A ...

C They all lived happily ever after.

A I'm hungry.

C I know.

A Can I eat some?

C Before Daddy? Well. Oh I'm sure he wouldn't mind a nibble
   before he

A Never tasted

C Open wide Train in the Isn't that?

   A vomits.

Oh darling no no It's Mummy's here to Go in the You sleep while

A I'm going for a drive

C Not when you're no

A Very short 'til

C Shall I wake Daddy before you?

A No need

C you'll see Daddy later, won't you?

A Course

C You won't go to the favela? I don't want you to go to the favela ever You'll be very careful

A I'm always

C Because you are the most precious thing that we

A I know

11.

A I brought you a

D Don't need

A gift Open your

D a gift

A If you Next time rich kid drives straight toward you Kid like What do you? Kill the kid Open the see it's I don't know much about Is it a good?

D Very

A the favela with a gun you can really

D Thank you

A You put a story in my head whispered my when I came here you told me the coup

D No memory at all of that

A You did a Really hurt me Which was right I'm scum We're all

D I don't need the gun

A Scum deserve to

D Take the

A I want

D Go home

A Because Tried to But always Once upon a Long time And then they So they Finally they Chatter Story Shoot me

D No

A Night. Exterior. Heat. Chav comes up the hill. Stop Cradle the gun in your Until you see the house My Pool lights casting the rippling over the That's a story Don't want Shoot me

D No

A We're sleeping safe in Maid's gone In her village her kid's
   You take out the dog He was going to bite at your Stop me
   please telling this Shoot me

D No

A dog floats in the pool bleeding in the You'll just hold up the
   pull the trigger pull easy

D No

A open the door Mummy Daddy fell asleep in front of Movie still
   Super heroes You call out the charges The world is yours Oh
   stop me hate this story no good stories any Shoot me Shoot

D No

A again again 'til Mummy's Daddy's brains are on the Fuck this
   in the Don't want to Just be silent The brains in my story
   are just if you shoot there'll be

D No

A Stop me telling this shitty

D No

A I'm woken by the Come rushing to You turn the weapon on
   I'm pleading for my Let me live let me see the green Where
   is this? Never stops coming from my mouth this story of
   Hurts always Imagination Mouth Pouring Make it How
   much longer do I SCUM CHAV I'll

   A *takes the gun.*

   Stop the You weep You can't I'm your Your long-lost
   Telenovela Structured Everything's

   A *puts down the gun.*

   I never I Talking forever.

   D *picks up the gun.*

D Pay the right price I'll

A Yes?

D Not today one day for the right price I'll

End

PROPS

Gun (p42)

SOUND EFFECTS

Recorded sobbing (p3)

A vomits (p40)

VISIT THE SAMUEL FRENCH BOOKSHOP AT THE ROYAL COURT THEATRE

Browse plays and theatre books, get expert advice and enjoy a coffee

Samuel French Bookshop
Royal Court Theatre
Sloane Square
London
SW1W 8AS
020 7565 5024

Shop from thousands of titles on our website

 samuelfrench.co.uk

 samuelfrenchltd

 samuel french uk

Lightning Source UK Ltd.
Milton Keynes UK
UKHW051015040719
345494UK00011B/176/P

Taking inspiration from Oedipus and Chilean children who were taken from their biological parents to support the Pinochet regime, *Golden Child* follows a young man's journey discovering that the people he knew to be his parents his whole life are not actually his parents.

| CASTING | 6 women or 6 men (flexible casting) |

SAMUEL FRENCH *Acting* Editions

✓ Clear text and large margins for practical use

✓ Choice of sizes and bindings to suit how you use playtexts

✓ Additional features help bring the play to life

ISBN 978-0-573-11607-0
90000

SAMUEL FRENCH